My Little Blue Book

First steps in Bible reading

Penny Boshoff

Scripture Union, 207–209 Queensway, Bletchley, Milton Keynes, MK2 2EB
Internet: www.scriptureunion.org.uk

Scripture Union is an international Christian charity working with churches in more than 130 countries providing resources to bring the good news about Jesus Christ to children, young people and families – and to encourage them to develop spiritually through the Bible and prayer.

As well as a network of volunteers, staff and associates who run holidays, church-based events and school Christian groups, Scripture Union produces a wide range of publications and supports those who use the resources through training programmes.

ISBN 978 1 85999 660 7

Scriptures quoted from the Contemporary English Version © American Bible Society 1991, 1992, 1995. Anglicisation © British & Foreign Bible Society 1996. Used with permission.

Illustrations: Jenny Tulip at Beehive Illustration Agency
Cover and internal design: Mark Carpenter Design Consultants
Additional material: Christine Wright
Rhyme on page 13 © Kathleen Crawford, from *Zac and the Multi-coloured Spidajig*, (SU). Reprinted with permission.
Typesetting: Servis Filmsetting Ltd, Manchester
Printed and bound by Henry Ling Ltd, Dorchester

What's in this book?

How to use this book

When children are small, before they can read, it can be hard to know how to introduce the Bible to them. The *Tiddlywinks Little Books* offer a simple and enjoyable way to do so. Each book introduces Bible stories and truths through the lives of young children today. As they explore and discover and learn about the Bible in their day-to-day lives, they share their discoveries with us.

There isn't a 'right' way to use *Tiddlywinks Little Books*. If you'd like to read something every day, each numbered page gives you a story and a prayer idea. Alternatively, you could read several pages in one go for a longer story. *Little Books* do not tie you to a certain date: use them as often as suits you and your child. Young children enjoy hearing stories again and again so don't feel you have to keep moving on or that you should only read a section once. There are extra pages too with ideas for activities, rhymes and craft, and things for the children to do themselves. There is also a page for you, as you seek to introduce ideas about God and the words of the Bible to the children in your care.

You might like to set aside a time for using the *Little Books*, perhaps at bedtime or while you have a meal together. Or keep the book handy so you can use it anytime – on a bus journey, at a pause in a day of busy playing or while you're waiting for a visitor to call.

Children in their early years are growing faster and learning more than at any other time in their lives – an ideal time to take their 'First steps into Bible reading'.

Meet Lucy and Liam

Come and meet Lucy and Liam. They are twins. They are three years old. But soon they will be four.

Lucy and Liam are always very busy. They love to play outside. Sometimes they play in their garden, sometimes they play in their grandad's garden and sometimes they go to the park. Lucy likes the swings best but Liam likes the climbing frame. He can climb right to the top.

When it is rainy and they can't play outside, the twins have lots of fun indoors. Liam loves making dens. He likes to be on his own in his den reading books, but he does let Lucy play too. Lucy's favourite rainy-day play is cutting and sticking. She cuts pictures out of magazines and sticks them in her special scrap book.

Every week, Lucy and Liam's cousin Reese comes to play. Every week Reese and the twins go to the Toddler Club at church. They have great fun playing, making things and learning new songs and rhymes. Liam likes the ones with actions.

With so much to do, so much to find out and so many games to play, let's turn the page and find out what Lucy and Liam are up to today…

*"Hello! I'm Tiddly Tim.
Look for me as you read this book!"*

Liam's itchy eye

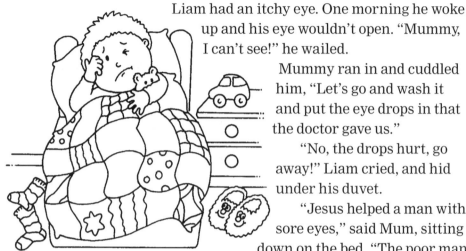

Liam had an itchy eye. One morning he woke up and his eye wouldn't open. "Mummy, I can't see!" he wailed.

Mummy ran in and cuddled him, "Let's go and wash it and put the eye drops in that the doctor gave us."

"No, the drops hurt, go away!" Liam cried, and hid under his duvet.

"Jesus helped a man with sore eyes," said Mum, sitting down on the bed. "The poor man had never been able to see. And they didn't have eye drops in those days. When Jesus saw him, he did something very strange. He mixed up some mud and put it on the man's eyes. 'Go and wash off the mud,' he said. The man did what Jesus told him and he could see everything!"

Liam peeped out, "Wow, will Jesus help me?"

Liam is very glad he has got eye drops to make his eye better!

Pray

Thank you Jesus for making the man's eyes better. Please help us too when we don't feel well.

John 9:1–34

Jesus helps a blind man

"Can you take this off now?" asked Lucy, tugging at her blindfold. She and Liam had been playing pirates, walking the plank. Lucy had tripped over the bricks box and landed on her bottom. Liam undid the blindfold. "Oh that's better!" Lucy said.

Do you think that's what the blind man said when Jesus made his eyes better? Everyone wanted to know how he could suddenly see. "Jesus did it," he said. "I did what Jesus said and now I can see."

Some people still didn't believe him. But the man who could see said to them, "We know that God listens only to people who love and obey him. This is the first time that anyone has given sight to someone born blind. Jesus could not do anything unless he came from God."

Pray

Jesus, you must be very special to make the man's eyes better.

"I'm reading"

"Read us a story!" Lucy and Liam shouted, climbing on to Daddy's lap.

"Mind my newspaper, you two – I'm reading!" Daddy replied.

Lucy frowned, "But you're not reading, Daddy. I can't hear you."

Daddy smiled, "That's because I can read in my head as well as out loud!"

This Bible story from Acts 8 is about a man who read aloud.

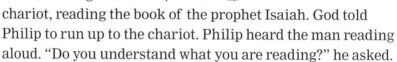

An important official was on his way home. He was sitting in his chariot, reading the book of the prophet Isaiah. God told Philip to run up to the chariot. Philip heard the man reading aloud. "Do you understand what you are reading?" he asked.

"No," replied the man. "How can I, unless someone helps me?"

"Did Philip help?" wondered Liam.

"Of course, Liam!" said Daddy.

Pray

The twins think it's fun to shout, whisper, talk and sing. Can you whisper?

Thank God for all the different sounds you can make.

Acts 8:26–40

Philip talks

Philip got into the chariot and sat by the important official. The man was reading part of the Bible, the book of Isaiah. "Tell me," he said, "was Isaiah talking about himself or about someone else?"

So Philip began at this place in the Bible and explained the good news about Jesus.

"Didn't the 'fishal' know Jesus?" asked Liam, as Daddy finished the story.

"No," explained Daddy. "The official was an important person at the Queen's palace in a country far away, so he hadn't met Jesus."

"Daddy, did Philip know Jesus?" asked Lucy.

"Yes, Lucy, he knew Jesus well. He was Jesus' friend, that's why he could tell the man all about him."

Pray

Who tells you about Jesus? Is it Mummy, Grandad or someone at your special group at church?

Thank you God for............................... who tells me all about Jesus.

Lucy's story

Lucy and Liam love to hear stories about Jesus making people well again. Lucy is going to tell us one of her favourites.

"One day, some people brought a deaf man who couldn't talk, to Jesus.

'Please make him well,' they asked.

Jesus took the man away from the crowd. Jesus touched the man's ears. Then he touched the man's tongue. Jesus looked up to heaven and said, 'Open up!' At once, the man could hear and talk."

"That's an exciting story, Lucy," said Mummy. "I wonder what the deaf man said when he could talk again?"

"I know," said Liam. "I think he said, 'Thank you!'"

Pray

Dear Jesus, you can do wonderful things. Thank you for making the deaf man well again.

Mark 7:31–37

Listen and hear

Lucy and Liam played the listening game in circle time when they went to Toddler Club. Would you like to play it too?

You have to sit very still, close your eyes and listen. What can you hear?

Look at the pictures. Point to the sounds you heard. Did you hear something different?

When Jesus healed the deaf man's ears, the man could hear straight away! Lucy thinks he heard birds singing. Liam thinks he heard his friends clapping and cheering. What do you think? The Bible tells us that the man heard lots of people in the crowd talking about Jesus, saying, **"Everything he does is good! He even heals people who cannot hear or talk."**

Pray

Talk about the different sounds you can hear. Isn't it clever how our ears can hear soft sounds as well as very loud ones?

Thank God for making ears so we can hear.

Mark 7:31–37　　　　11

Lucy and Liam's spots!

Mummy was helping Lucy and Liam to get dressed. "Oh dear!" she sighed. "I think you've both got chickenpox."

The twins looked at each other. Their tummies were covered in spots.

"I'd better phone Auntie Lindsay. Chickenpox is catching so Reese won't be able to come to play today. You can play with him when all your spots have gone."

"It's not fair," groaned the twins.

In Jesus' time, people with skin diseases had to keep away from everyone. Nobody touched, hugged or even talked to them.

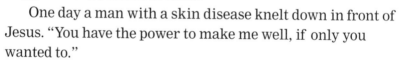

One day a man with a skin disease knelt down in front of Jesus. "You have the power to make me well, if only you wanted to."

What do you think Jesus did?

Jesus put his hand on the man and said, "I want to!"

Pray

Dear Jesus, the man must have felt very lonely. I'm glad you wanted to touch him and make him well.

Matthew 8:1–4

Move it!

Clap your hands, touch your toes,

Clean your teeth, blow your nose.

Click your fingers, stretch up high,

Say "Hello" or wave goodbye.

Switch on the light, open a door,

Dig the garden, sweep the floor.

Bake a cake, then eat your tea,

Bounce a ball or skip with me.

Drive a car, row a boat,

Scratch an itch, fasten your coat.

Hug a teddy, stroke the cat,

Brush your hair, put on a hat.

Paint a picture, write your name,

Build a tower, play a game.

Open a parcel or a jar,

Bang a drum, play a guitar.

Our hands

Lucy was crying and Liam was sulking in the corner, holding a toy rabbit.

"What happened?" asked Mummy.

"He snatched Pinky and he thumped me," wailed Lucy.

"She pushed me!" complained Liam.

"Liam, give Pinky back to Lucy," said Mummy. "Then say sorry and give each other a hug."

Jesus didn't thump or push, he used his hands to make people feel better. The man with sore skin was always being told to go away. Nobody wanted him near them. He expected Jesus to send him away too.

But Jesus didn't do that. He reached out and touched him and made his skin better, just like that!

Jesus wants us to be kind, too. Lucy and Liam are going to try not to push or thump or pinch each other. Liam says he won't snatch Pinky again and Lucy says they can share Pinky and play with him together.

Pray

Hands can wave and hands can clap, hands can thump and hands can snatch, hands can push and hands can shove, hands can stroke and hands can love, hands can pat and hands can share. Jesus wants our hands to care.

Can you make up some actions to go with these words

Matthew 8:1–4

Liam's "orange" juice

"My orange juice tastes funny," complained Liam.

Lucy made a face, "Ugh, so does mine!"

Mummy tasted Liam's drink. She disappeared into the kitchen and came back with the bottle of squash. "No wonder it tastes funny. I bought tropical squash instead of orange! Would you like some blackcurrant instead?"

What drink do you like best?

In Jesus' day, they liked to drink wine, especially at parties. Once, when Jesus was at a party, all the wine ran out. Jesus told the servants to fill six enormous jars to the top with water. "Take some water to the man in charge," Jesus said.

When the man tasted his cup of water, it had turned into wine! "This is the best wine I have tasted!" he said.

Pray

Some drinks are cold, and some drinks are hot, lemonade is fizzy, milk is not, apple juice is yellow, grapefruit juice is pink. Thank you God for all these drinks.

John 2:1–10   15

Poor Lucy

Can you see what's wrong with Lucy? She fell out of Grandad's apple tree and broke her leg. She can't walk or run. But the doctor says her leg will be better soon.

This Bible story is about a man who couldn't walk.

Peter and John were going to talk to God at a special place called the temple. There was a man sitting by the temple door. This man had never been able to walk. He begged people who were going in to give him money.

"Give me a few pennies!"

Peter looked at him, "I don't have any money, but I will give you something else. In the name of Jesus Christ, get up and start walking." Peter held the man's hand and helped him up. At once, the man started walking!

Pray

Do you know someone who can't walk very well – an older person or someone who has a disability or is in hospital? Talk to God about them.

Acts 3:1–10

"I can move"

Lucy and her mummy were waiting at the hospital. Lucy was very quiet. "Aren't you happy about the nurse taking your cast off?" Mummy asked.

"Yes," Lucy looked a bit scared. "But will it hurt?"

"No, the nurse will be very gentle," Mummy said.

Do you remember Peter helping the man who couldn't walk?

When Peter held the man's hand and helped him up, the man's feet and ankles became strong. He jumped up and started walking. He went with Peter and John into the temple. He was walking and jumping and praising God for making him well.

Lucy was like the man in the Bible story. She was full of energy, trying to skip and run. She shouted, "Look at me, Mummy!"

Can you hop and jump?

Pray

Look God, I can walk and I can run, see me climbing – it's such fun! I can balance, can you see? Hop, skip, jump... one, two, three!

Acts 3:1–11

Let's move!

Lucy and Liam would like to teach you this action rhyme.

Peter and John went to pray,   *(Hands together.)*
They met a lame man on the way.   *(Move arms as if walking.)*
He asked for gold as he held out his hands   *(Hold out hands.)*
And this is what Peter did say,
"Silver and gold have I none   *(Shake head.)*
But such as I have I give you –   *(Giving action.)*
In the name of Jesus Christ   *(Point upwards.)*
Of Nazareth, rise up and walk." *(Stand up and walk on the spot.)*
He went walking...   *(Walk on spot.)*
    and leaping...   *(Jump in the air.)*
        and praising God,   *(Lift arms upwards.)*
Walking...   *(Walk on spot.)*
    and leaping...   *(Jump in the air.)*
        and praising God.   *(Lift arms upwards.)*
"In the name of Jesus Christ   *(Point upwards.)*
Of Nazareth, rise up and walk!" *(Stand up and walk on the spot.)*

Acts 3:1–11

Solomon's dream

Mummy was reading the twins a story from the Bible about a man called Solomon.

Solomon was not very old when he became king. One night, God spoke to Solomon in a dream.

"Ask for anything you want, and I will give it to you," God said.

Solomon thought hard. "Lord God, I'm your servant but I'm very young. I don't know how to lead your people," he said. "Please make me wise. Teach me the difference between right and wrong. Then I will be a good king."

God was very pleased with Solomon. "I'll make you wiser than anyone who has ever lived," God promised.

"What does wise mean?" asked Lucy.

"Well, being wise meant that Solomon always knew the right thing to do. He knew what would make God happy."

"Like sharing?" wondered Lucy.

What do you think? Talk about other things that make God happy. Sharing your toys? Being kind? Helping?

Pray

Dear God, I want to do things that make you happy. Please help me to

....

Thank you.

1 Kings 3:1–15; 2 Chronicles 1:1–12   19

Lucy's horse

One Saturday morning Daddy, Lucy and Liam were playing with play dough. "I'm making a digger," Liam announced.

"Mine's going to be a horse," said Lucy.

A little while later, Lucy threw her horse on the floor. She burst into tears. "It won't go!" she cried angrily. "I hate play dough. I'm not going to play anymore!"

Have you ever tried to make something and it didn't come out right?

Jeremiah wrote in the Bible about the day he saw a potter making pots out of clay. Whenever the clay didn't turn into the shape he wanted, the potter would change his mind and make it into a different shape.

"I am like the potter," God said to Jeremiah. "I make people. They are all special to me. Even when they go wrong, I can make them right again."

Daddy picked up Lucy's play dough horse. "This is a really good elephant!" he smiled. "Make a trunk for him, Lucy."

Pray

What do you like best? Cutting and sticking? Painting? Play dough?

"Dear God, I like making things. I like

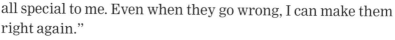

.... best."

The potter's jar has broken. Can you find the piece to mend it?

Play clay

Ask a grown-up to use this recipe to make some play clay.

You will need:

    1 cup of cornflour
    1¼ cups of cold water
    2 cups of bicarbonate of soda

What to do:

1. Mix all the ingredients in a saucepan.
2. Stir over medium heat for 4 minutes until the mixture thickens.
3. Remove from the heat, turn the mixture onto a plate and cover with a damp cloth until cool.
4. Knead the play clay until smooth.

Make a pot, or maybe an animal like Lucy and Liam did.

Making me

Lucy was very pleased with her play dough elephant. Liam couldn't wait to show Mummy the digger he had made.

"What shall I make?" Daddy asked.

"A dumper truck!" Liam shouted.

"A giraffe!" cried Lucy.

"Hmm, I think I'll make a snail," said Daddy.

"No, Daddy!" Lucy and Liam shouted.

"But it's my bit of play dough," said Daddy. "So I'll decide what to make!"

God decided to make you and me. In the Bible, God says, "You are in my hands, just like clay in the potter's hands". God wants us to know that we belong to him. He wants to make us into lovely people. Sometimes we do wrong things, which makes God sad. But God can help us do the things that make him happy instead.

Pray

Dear God, thank you for making me. I'm glad I belong to you.

Jeremiah 18:1–17

A sweet smell

Lucy loves the smell of her mummy's perfume.
Sometimes, when Mummy is getting ready to
go out, she puts a bit of perfume on Lucy too.
One day, Lucy decided to put some perfume on
when Mummy wasn't there. Lucy was trying to
be careful but the perfume spilt on the carpet.
"If I hide the bottle, Mummy won't
know," Lucy thought. But her mummy
found out because the whole bedroom
smelt of perfume!

A woman in the Bible spilt some
perfume, but it wasn't an accident.

Mary opened a very expensive bottle
of perfume. She poured it on Jesus' feet.
She wiped his feet with her hair. The
sweet smell of the perfume filled the house.

Mary did this to show Jesus how much she loved him.

Pray

You can do all sorts of things to show
Jesus you love him. You can sing him your
favourite song or paint a special picture.
Tell him in words, out loud or in your
head.

John 12:1–8   23

A lovely smell

Lucy and Liam's cousin Reese had come to play.

"It smells nice in here," he said. "It's Mummy's perfume," explained Liam. "Lucy was naughty and spilt it and Mummy got cross."

"I said sorry," said Lucy.

Have a look at the Bible story in John 12. It's the story of Mary who spilt the perfume. Some people got cross with her.

A friend of Jesus, called Judas, was there. "Why wasn't this perfume sold for three hundred silver coins and the money given to the poor people?" he said crossly.

"Leave Mary alone!" said Jesus. "She has kept this perfume specially for me."

Mummy was tucking Lucy up in bed. "Are you still cross with me, Mummy?" Lucy asked.

"No, I know you didn't mean to do it and I know you're sorry. And…" Mummy gave her a big hug, "…I love you very much."

Lucy's prayer

Dear Jesus, I'm sorry when I do things that make other people cross. I'm glad that you love me even when I've been naughty.

Liam is growing

"Liam your trousers are getting too short!" exclaimed Mummy. "You've grown again!"

"Can you measure us?" Lucy and Liam said excitedly. They ran to the special chart on their bedroom door. Mummy helped to measure them.

Can you see who is taller?

How do you know how much you have grown? Do your clothes get shorter like Liam's? Maybe you have a special chart too?

Samuel was a little boy when he went to live at God's house, the temple. He helped Eli, the priest, serve God. Samuel wore a special linen tunic and the clothes his mother made for him. Samuel soon grew out of his clothes, so his mother would make new clothes for him every year.

Pray

"I used to be a baby, then I grew / a little bit bigger and not so new. / I learnt to crawl and then to walk / and after that I learnt to talk. / I know I'm growing 'cos my clothes get smaller, / my legs get longer and I get taller. / I'm going to be a big *girl/boy* soon, I know, / so thank you God for helping me grow!"

1 Samuel 3　　　　　　　　　　　　　　　　　　　25

God talks to Samuel

Liam's Bible has a picture of a little boy, called Samuel, asleep in his bed.

One night Samuel was sleeping when God called out, "Samuel!"

Samuel ran to Eli and said, "Here I am!"

"I didn't call you," Eli answered. "Go back to sleep."

God called Samuel three times. Each time Samuel ran to Eli and each time Eli said. "Go back to sleep."

God hadn't spoken to Samuel before so Samuel didn't recognise his voice. At last, Eli realised that it was God who was calling. He told Samuel, "If someone calls you again, say, 'I'm listening Lord. What do you want me to do?'"

The next time God called, Samuel replied, "I'm listening Lord. What do you want me to do?"

"I want you to give special messages to the people for me," said God.

Pray

Dear God, I am glad you kept calling Samuel. Help me to hear you and be ready to do what you ask me.

Elisha's new room

Do you have a bedroom all to yourself? Or do you share? Lucy and Liam share their bedroom but soon they will have a room each. Mummy and Daddy are making a room in the loft.

"Elisha had a new room too," Daddy said, picking up the Bible. "He used to visit a woman and her husband in a town called Shunem. One day, the woman said, "I'm sure Elisha is God's special messenger. **Why don't we build Elisha a small room on the flat roof of our house? We can put a bed, a table and chair and an oil lamp in it. Then whenever he comes, he can stay with us.**"

Is your room like Elisha's? Do you have a bed? A table? A chair? A lamp? Do you have things in your room that Elisha didn't have?

Pray

Tell God all about your room. Thank him for all the things you like.

2 Kings 4:8–17

Lucy tidies up

Lucy is very tidy. One day she had put away all her toys and had nearly finished putting the books back on the shelf. Liam came in. "Is my 'Thomas' book there?" he asked, pulling all the books out on the floor.

"Liam!" wailed Lucy, "I was tidying them and you've messed it all up. Mummy, Liam's messed everything up!"

"Never mind," said Mummy, "soon you will have your own room. Won't that be lovely?"

Elisha was very pleased with his new room. He wanted to thank the woman who had made it for him. "How can I help you?" he asked.

"I have everything I need," she replied.

Later, Elisha found out that she didn't have any children. "Next year, you'll have a baby son," Elisha promised. And that is exactly what happened!

Pray

Dear God, thank you for my home.
I like it because

....

2 Kings 4:8–17

Find the odd one out

Can you find the odd one out in each row?

Now colour them all in.

A surprise for Lucy and Liam

The twins and Mummy were just leaving to go to play in the park when the postman brought a big parcel with Liam and Lucy's names on it. "It's from Granny," said Mummy, giving the excited twins the parcel. Liam tore open the paper. There were two jumpers – a pink one with blue stripes and a red one with green stripes. "What lovely jumpers! Isn't Granny clever?" Mummy said.

"Can we wear them now?" asked Liam.

Can you guess which jumper was Liam's and which was Lucy's?

Dorcas was like Lucy and Liam's Granny – she made coats and clothes for other people. She was always doing good things for everyone and she was especially kind to poor people. You can read all about her in the Bible.

Pray

Do you have a favourite jumper? Or a favourite coat? What colour is it? Tell God what you like to wear.

Acts 9:36–40

Busy Dorcas

Jo was telling all the children at Toddler Club the story of Dorcas.

"Dorcas lived in a town called Joppa. She was always making clothes and helping people."

"Like my granny?" asked Lucy. "She made my jumper. And Liam's."

Jo smiled, "Yes, I like the stripes. Do you think Dorcas made stripy clothes? One day, Dorcas became ill and died. Her friends went to Peter. 'Please come with us as quickly as you can!' they asked him. They took Peter to the room where Dorcas lay. Then they showed him the coats and clothes that Dorcas had made while she was still alive. Peter knelt down and prayed. He asked Jesus to make Dorcas well again. Then he turned to Dorcas. 'Get up , Dorcas!' he said. Dorcas opened her eyes and sat up. Dorcas was alive again! Just think how happy Dorcas' friends were! Who do you think made Dorcas better?"

"I know!" called out Liam. "It was Jesus!"

Pray

Jesus, thank you that you can do anything!

Acts 9:36–40

Where does your food come from?

Lucy and Liam go to the supermarket to buy their cereal for breakfast. They buy fruit and vegetables from the market. They buy chicken and sausages from the butcher. Sometimes Grandad brings them lettuces from his allotment. In the autumn, there are always apples from the tree in Grandad's garden.

God's special people were travelling through the desert. There were no shops and nothing around to eat. "We're hungry," they complained to their leader, Moses.

God said to Moses, "I have heard my people complaining. Tell them that I will feed them. Each evening they will have meat to eat. Each morning they will have more than enough bread."

God made sure they had enough to eat. And God provides food for us too.

Pray

Why not sing this prayer at meal times to the tune of 'Twinkle, twinkle, little star'?
Thank you for our food today.
Help us love you Lord, we pray.

                                    Exodus 16:3–10

Pancake Day!

We have special food on special occasions. Lucy and Liam have pancakes on Shrove Tuesday. Do you? They like to watch their Mummy toss the pancakes in the air.

Shrove Tuesday is the beginning of getting ready for Easter, when we remember that Jesus died to make us friends with God again.

Look at the food in the picture. When would you eat each of these?

Every year at the Passover festival, God's special people, the Israelites, remembered how God rescued

them. God told his people to eat roast lamb and flat bread on the night before their escape.

"When you eat the meal be dressed and ready to travel," God said. "Have your sandals on, carry your walking stick and eat quickly. This is the Passover festival in honour of me, your God."

Pray

Dear God, I like the special days you give us. I like ....
best because ....

Getting ready for a party

The twins will be four soon. "Who shall we invite to your birthday party?" Mummy asked. "Reese!" both children shouted.

"And Josh and Ben," said Liam.

"Can Krista and Lily and Hannah come?" asked Lucy.

Parties are fun when lots of friends come.

Jesus told a story about a man who was giving a big party. He had invited a lot of people. His servant went to tell the guests, "Everything is ready! Please come to the party."

One by one each of the guests made excuses. "I can't come," said one. "I'm too busy," said another.

The man was upset that his friends would not come to his party. He said to his servant, "Go to every street. Bring everyone who is poor or disabled, blind or who can't walk. Bring lots of people in, so that my house will be full."

Pray

Jesus liked parties. Do you? What do you like best about parties? Tell Jesus.

Luke 14:15–24

The best party ever

Liam wants to tell you all about their birthday party.

"I helped Daddy blow up balloons. One of them went BANG! Lucy found the crisps and ate some and Mummy got cross. Then I put my blue shirt on and Lucy put on her long red dress. Then everyone came. There were lots of presents and cards. We played Musical Bumps and Pass the Parcel. And I had a 'Thomas' Cake with four candles. Everyone sang 'Happy birthday'. I blew all the candles out. It was the best day ever!"

Jesus said, "People will come from everywhere and sit down to a wonderful party in God's kingdom." The party that we will have with Jesus one day will be even better than the best party you have ever been to!

Liam's Prayer

I love parties, Jesus. I'm glad we will have a party with you one day.

Liam's fun day

Liam's and Lucy's grandparents sometimes take them for special trips. Liam's favourite day out was when Grandad took him on a steam train just like Thomas the Tank Engine. Grandad took a photo of Liam in the driver's cab. Liam put it on his bedroom wall.

Have you had a special day out? Where did you go?

God says it's good for us to have a rest from the things we do every day. When God made the earth, he worked very hard. When he had finished, he thought it was all very good so he rested.

In the Bible it says, **God blessed the seventh day and made it special because on that day he rested from his work**.

Pray

Thank you God for rest and play,
Thank you God for special days.

Genesis 2:1–3

Party time!

Party straws
Cut a shape out of coloured card. Decorate with glitter-glue or crayons. Punch holes in the top and bottom and thread a bendy straw through the holes. Then use with your favourite juice!

Crispie treats
You will need:
5 cups of popped rice cereal
¼ cup of butter or margarine
4 cups of marshmallows
Food colouring
A grown-up to help you

What to do:
1 Melt the margarine in a saucepan.
2 Add the marshmallows and cook over a low heat, stirring all the time until the mixture is syrupy.
3 Add food colouring if you wish and stir well.
4 Remove from heat, add the cereal and stir well.
5 Press the mixture into a baking tray and let it cool.
6 Use pastry cutters to cut out interesting shapes.

Animal round-up
Cut out lots of pictures of birds, farm animals and zoo animals. Make large pictures of a nest, a farm and a zoo. Scatter the animal pictures around the room. How quickly can you get all the animals to their right homes?

Traffic lights
You will need lots of space for this game. The leader starts by saying, "The traffic is going slowly (crawling, zooming)." As soon as the leader says, "Green light," you go around the room slowly (crawling or zooming). When the leader says, "Red Light," you must stop straightaway.

Tasty necklaces
Make necklaces or bracelets out of sweets! Thread sweets or cereal with holes in onto string liquorice or jelly strings. Get a grown-up to help you tie them on, then munch away!

Party tablecloth
Decorate your own party tablecloth. Cover your party table with a long sheet of paper – plain wallpaper is great. Set the table with your party plates and cups (don't forget your special straws) and give everyone some crayons to draw on your paper tablecloth!

Going fishing

Lucy and Liam were on holiday by the seaside. One morning, Daddy took them to the harbour to watch the fishing boats unload their fish. The fishermen were very busy. One of them smiled at the twins. He held up a big fish. "This tastes really good with chips," he said.

"Jesus' friends were fishermen," said Daddy later at home. "Jesus was walking along the shore of Lake Galilee, when he saw two brothers, Peter and Andrew. They were fishermen. They were holding their nets in the lake to catch fish. 'Come with me!' Jesus said. 'I will teach you how to bring in people instead of fish.' At once the brothers put down their nets, left everything and went with Jesus."

"Do I have to be a fishermen to be Jesus' friend?" asked Lucy.

"No, anyone can be a friend of Jesus," said Daddy.

Pray

Jesus, I'm glad I can be your friend, just like Peter and Andrew.

Matthew 4:18–22

Four friends for Jesus

A long time ago, there were four fishermen – Peter and his
brother Andrew, and James and his brother John. One day,
Jesus was walking along the beach. Peter and Andrew were
fishing. James and John were in a boat mending the
fishing nets. "Come and be my friends!" Jesus
called to them. At once they left their boats and
nets. They wanted to be friends with Jesus.

Who is your best friend? Liam has drawn
a picture of his best friend. Can you see who
it is?

Yes, Lucy! He says he likes Lucy because
they play hide and seek together. What do you
like doing with your friends? Jesus and
his friends spent lots of time together,
talking, walking, and eating lunch and tea
together.

Pray

Find a photo or draw a picture of your
friend. Put it on your bedroom wall and
talk to Jesus about your friend whenever
you look at it.

Matthew 4:18–22   39

The Trusting Soldier

Lucy and Liam learnt this "Trusting Soldier" rhyme at Toddler Club. Let's say it with them. Don't forget the actions.

Important people came to Jesus.
"Please help our friend," they begged.   *(Hands together.)*
"Our friend the soldier is so kind.   *(Salute.)*
Now his servant is ill in bed."   *(Hands make a pillow.)*

As Jesus set off for the soldier's house,   *(Salute.)*
A messenger ran up and said,   *(Mime running.)*
"My master the soldier said, 'Just give the word   *(Salute.)*
And my servant will leap out of bed.'"   *(Jump in the air.)*

Jesus was pleased. "What a wonderful thing   *(Clap.)*
To find someone who trusts me so well."   *(Hands open.)*
From that moment on the servant was healed!   *(Jump in air.)*
What a great story he had to tell!

Pray

Jesus, you are amazing to make the servant well, just like that!

Luke 7:1–10

Jesus is pleased

"I like the 'Soldier' rhyme," said Liam, saluting.

"So do I," said Lucy, jumping in the air, "but why does it say Jesus was pleased?"

"Let's have a look at the story," said Mummy going to find the Bible. "Here it is, in Luke chapter 7. The soldier said '**Lord, don't go to any trouble for me! I am not good enough for you to come in to my house. … Just say the word, and my servant will get well**.' I think the soldier knew Jesus was special. He knew Jesus didn't have to see or touch the servant to make him well. Jesus could just say 'Get well' and it would happen!"

"That's good, isn't it Mummy!" Lucy said. "Let's do the 'Soldier' rhyme again!"

Pray

Jesus, help me to remember that you are special and that you can do wonderful things.

Luke 7:1–10

Money, money, money

Grandad was playing shops with Lucy and
Liam. Lucy was the shopkeeper. She
was putting all the money in piles.
"I think I'll call you Matthew!"
Grandad said.

"But my name's Lucy!"

"Yes, I know," Grandad
laughed, "but you are
counting out your money just
like Jesus' friend, Matthew."

"Oh," said Lucy, "was he
a shopkeeper too?"

"No, he worked for the
Romans, collecting lots of money from people. Nobody liked
the Romans. Nobody liked Matthew either."

"Did Jesus like him?" Liam asked.

"Oh yes. Jesus asked Matthew to be one of his special
friends. Shall we look the story up in your Bible?"

You can look up the story too. It's in Matthew 9:9–13. Can
you find Matthew's name? It begins with "M".

Pray

Jesus, sometimes people are horrid to me.
Help me remember you're always there.
Sometimes people say nasty things. Help
me remember you always care.

Matthew 9:9–13

A friend for Matthew

Lucy was sitting on Grandad's lap. They were reading about Matthew in Lucy's Bible.

"I want to sit on your lap too, Grandad!" moaned Liam.

"No I'm here!" Lucy said. "Go away!"

"Lucy, don't be horrid to Liam. There's lots of room for him too," said Grandad, helping Liam on to his lap.

Lucy didn't want to share Grandad's lap. Some people didn't want to share Jesus either. They didn't want Jesus to be friends with Matthew. "Why does Jesus eat with money-collectors and people who do wrong things?" they complained one day, when Jesus was having dinner at Matthew's house.

"I came to help people like Matthew," replied Jesus. "You have to learn that God wants you to be kind to others."

Pray

Jesus, I'm sorry when I'm horrid. You are always kind. Please help me to be kind too.

Matthew 9:9–13

Martha and Mary

If Jesus came to your house what would you do? Lucy and Liam say that they would play with Jesus in their den.

One day, Jesus went to Martha and Mary's house.

Martha welcomed Jesus. She had a sister, Mary. Mary sat down by Jesus and was listening to what he said. Martha was worried about all the cooking and work that had to be done. At last she said to Jesus, "**Lord, doesn't it bother you that my sister Mary has left me to do all the work by myself? Tell her to come and help me!**"

"Martha," Jesus answered, "you are worried about so many things, but only one thing is really important. Mary has chosen what is best."

Which sister listened to Jesus?

Pray

Mary sat close to listen to Jesus,
Martha had too much to do.
Make me like Mary, ready to listen,
Quietly learning from you.

44   **Luke 10:38–42**

First steps in Bible reading

The *Tiddlywinks* range of Little Books

My Little Red Book
First steps in Bible reading
Reese discovers Christmas is coming...
978 1 85999 659 1

My Little Yellow Book
First steps in Bible reading
Danny finds out about Easter.
1 85999 693 0

My Little Blue Book
First steps in Bible reading
Lucy and Liam find out All about me...
978 1 85999 660 7

My Little Green Book
First steps in Bible reading
Krista explores God's wonderful world
1 85999 696 5

My Little Orange Book
First steps in Bible reading
Jamie looks inside God's big book.
1 85999 717 1

My Little Purple Book
First steps in Bible reading
Lily discovers 'Jesus loves me'.
1 85999 720 1

Tiddlywinks Little Books are designed to be used at home by a parent/carer with an individual child. Linked to the themes covered in the *Tiddlywinks* Big Books, children can discover and learn about the Bible and share their discoveries with you. There are 50 first steps in Bible reading pages in each book, with a story for each day and extra activity pages of fun things to do. Children will love exploring the Bible with child characters Lucy and Liam, Reese, Danny, Krista, Lily and Jamie.
A5, 64pp £3.50 each (Prices subject to change)

You can order these or any other *Tiddlywinks* resources from:
● Your local Christian bookstore
● Scripture Union Mail Order:
  Telephone 0845 07 06 006
● Online: log on to
  www.scriptureunion.org.uk/tiddlywinks
  to order securely from our online bookshop

" When the Big Books are used in conjunction with the Little Books, children and adults encounter an attractive mixture of stories and activities that will encourage everybody to know and trust in Jesus. *"*
Diana Turner,
Editor of *Playleader Magazine*

Tiddlywinks
The flexible resource for pre-school children and carers

Also now on sale!
Glitter and Glue. Pray and Play.
Even more craft and prayer ideas for use with under fives

Listen!

At Toddler Club, Jo was telling the
story of Jesus at Martha and Mary's
house. Lucy and Liam were
giggling and poking each other.

"Liam, Lucy, are you
listening?" asked Jo. "Lucy,
can you come and help me
tell the story? You too,
Liam? I need someone to
hold this picture of Mary,
sitting and listening to
Jesus, and someone to hold
the picture of Martha, busy getting the lunch ready."

The twins held up the pictures. Jo continued the story.

"Martha wasn't happy. 'I'm doing all the work Jesus. It
isn't fair!' she said.

'Martha, don't get so upset over things that aren't
important. The most important thing is to listen to me,' said
Jesus."

Where do you have to sit still and listen? At pre-school? At
story time at the library?

Pray

Dear Jesus, I like stories but sometimes it's
hard to sit so still and listen. Please help
me.

　　　　　　　　　　　　　　Luke 10:38–42

The man by the pool

My name is Reuben. I've been ill for a very long time. My legs and arms don't work properly. I often come to this special pool. Lots of sick and disabled people come here. We wait beside the pool for the water to start moving. If you get in the pool at that moment it can make you better. I've been waiting a long time, but nobody helps me get in when the water moves and my body is too slow. I always miss out. It's not fair.

"It wasn't fair when I missed my turn on the trampoline." said Liam to Mummy. "I waited and waited."

"I know," said Mummy. "How did you feel?"

"I cried, I was very, very sad," sighed Liam.

Pray

Have you ever missed your turn? Have you ever waited for something and it didn't happen? Tell Jesus how you felt.

Jesus heals

What makes you better when you are ill?

There was a man beside the pool who had been sick for 38 years. When Jesus saw the man and realised he had been disabled for such a long time, he asked, "Do you want to get well?"

"Yes, Lord. But I don't have anyone to help me into the pool when the water is stirred up. I try to get in but someone else always gets there first."

Jesus told him, "Pick up your mat and walk!"

At once the man was healed. He picked up his mat and started walking around.

Lucy says, "Isn't Jesus wonderful! The man didn't have any medicine. Jesus made him better just like that!"

Pray

Do you know anyone who is ill? We can ask Jesus to help them get well.

Dear Jesus, you do wonderful things.

Please make .... better.

Noah's boat

Liam and Grandad were playing with Grandad's big wooden Noah's ark. Grandad was telling the story.

"God was sad. Nobody listened to him. Only Noah did what God said.

'There is too much badness, Noah,' said God. 'I'm going to get rid of it all. You must build a really big boat, with a roof and a door on one side. Cover it inside and out with tar so the water can't get in. I am going to send a flood to destroy everything, but I'll keep you and your family safe. Take a male and female of each kind of bird, animal and reptile with you. You need to store enough food on the boat for you and all the animals.' And that's what Noah did."

"Grandad, what tools did Noah use?" Liam asked.

What do you think?

What sort of food did the animals eat?

Pray

Dear God, I'm glad you wanted to keep Noah and the animals safe. My favourite animal is

....

Genesis 6:8 – 8:19   49

It's raining!

Lucy and Liam were playing at Grandad and Grandma's house. They wanted to play in the garden but it was pouring with rain.

"When it stops, you can go out," Grandma promised.

"It's never going to stop!" moaned Lucy, looking out of the window.

Noah must have thought the rain would never stop too! The rain poured down for forty days and forty nights without stopping. The water became deeper and deeper. The boat started to float. Finally the flood was so deep even the highest mountain was under water.

In the Bible it says: **God did not forget about Noah and the animals with him in the boat. So God made a wind blow, and the water started going down.**

Pray

God sends the rain and God sends the sun.
Inside and outside we play and have fun!

Genesis 6:8 – 8:19

Help the animals into the boat

Can you help the kangaroo, parrot and snake find the other one of their pair so they can get into the boat?

Noah's boat full of animals

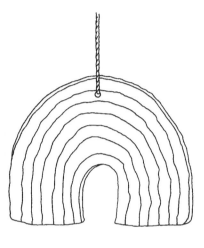

"Is the land dry yet?" Noah asked one day.
"Yes," said God. "Come on out and pray."

Every foot, hoof and paw,
Every trotter and claw,
Hurried out of the boat to the ground.

"Will it rain so hard again?" Noah wanted
  to know.
"No," said God. "I've made a rainbow."

"The red and the yellow
And the green and the blue
Are there in the sky as a sign to you.
I promise I'll not send so much rain
To destroy all creatures ever again."

Liam and Lucy have been making a rainbow mobile to hang
in their room. You could make one too!

Ask someone to help you draw the shape of a rainbow,
colour it in, cut it out and hang it in your room.

Pray

Dear God, I'm glad that you will never
send another flood to cover the earth.
I know you keep your promises.

Genesis 6:8 – 8:19

The walls of Jericho

At Toddler Club, the children were making a wall out of cardboard boxes. "It needs to be big like the wall in our Bible story today," Jo said. Liam stood on a stool to put the last box on top.

"The city walls of Jericho were very high and thick – even higher than our wall!" said Jo. "Joshua had to get over the walls to defeat the city. It was going to be difficult.

'I will help you,' God said to Joshua. 'This is what you must do. March around Jericho once a day for six days. On the seventh day, march seven times around the city. When the priests blow the trumpets, everyone must shout. The walls will fall down immediately.'

Joshua was very glad God was going to help them."

Pray

Dear God, help me remember that you will always help me when I have to do difficult things.

The trumpet march

"Let's pretend we're God's people and march around our wall," said Jo. "Joshua told seven priests to march in front playing trumpets. Who wants to do that?" Lucy and Liam put up their hands. Jo handed them each a recorder. "We'll pretend the recorders are our trumpets. Krista, Lily, Danny and Ben can carry the special box. The rest of us will march slowly behind them. Everyone must be quiet except the people playing trumpets." Everyone marched. When they stopped, Lucy and Liam blew their "trumpets" really loudly.

"On the seventh day they marched around Jericho seven times. When we get to seven everyone must shout. One... two... three... four..."

The children marched quietly. "five... six... seven!"

"RAAAAAAH!" they all shouted. And with a little help, the cardboard wall came tumbling down just like the walls of

Pray

God promised he would help his people and he did!

Thank you God for always keeping your promises.

Joshua at Jericho

"March around Jericho slowly," said God,
"Put the priests with the trumpets ahead.
Make sure you carry the special box
And don't say a word!" God said.

The people marched quietly round each day.
Just once, then they went back to bed.
Then on the seventh day it all changed.
"March seven times around," God said.

The people marched and marched and marched,
They marched and marched some more,
They marched 'til they heard the trumpets blow,
Then they shouted 'til their voices were sore.

A mumble and a rumble and grumble were heard,
Then CRASH! There came a huge sound!
And the great city walls of Jericho
Came tumbling down to the ground!

Apple picking

Lucy and Liam like helping Grandma pick up the apples that fall from the tree. Grandma gives them each a box. The twins work very hard filling their boxes. Who has picked the most apples?

A long time ago there were two women, Ruth and Naomi. They didn't have anything to eat so Ruth went out to the harvest fields. "Can I pick up the grain that the harvest workers drop?" she asked. The man who owned the field was called Boaz. He saw how hard Ruth worked. He knew that Ruth was very kind to Naomi.

"May God reward you for being so kind to Naomi," Boaz said to Ruth.

Boaz made sure Ruth went back home with a large basket full of grain.

Pray

Every time I help someone, God is glad.
Every time that I am kind, God is glad.

Ruth marries Boaz

Mummy and Daddy were going out. Lucy was watching
Mummy get ready. Mummy was putting on some perfume.
 "Please put some perfume on me," Lucy said. "I want to
smell nice like you."
 One day, Naomi told Ruth to get ready to go out to meet
Boaz. "It's time I found you a husband who will give you a
home and take care of you," Naomi decided. "Put on some
perfume and wear your best clothes. I'll tell you what you
must say to Boaz."
 Ruth did what Naomi asked. When
Ruth saw Boaz, she said, "I am
Ruth. You belong to Naomi's
family so you should take
care of us."
 So Boaz married Ruth
and they had a baby boy.
Naomi was so happy.
 Do you know people
who are married? Talk to
God about them.

Pray

Dear God, please make

....

as happy as Ruth and Boaz.

The shepherd king

Have you ever been chosen to do something special? Liam was chosen to be a shepherd in the Christmas play. He was happy but a bit scared too.

God said to Samuel, "Go and see Jesse. I've chosen one of his sons to be king."

When Samuel arrived he saw Eliab. "He's tall and handsome. He must be the one God has chosen," thought Samuel.

"No," said God. "I haven't chosen him."

Then Samuel saw Abinadab. God hadn't chosen him either.

Samuel saw five more sons. "God hasn't chosen any of these," Samuel said to Jesse. "Do you have any more?"

"My youngest son, David, is looking after the sheep," said Jesse.

When David came, God said, "He's the one I have chosen!"

I wonder how David felt? Talk about being chosen for different things (holding the biscuit plate at nursery, talking to the group at circle time).

Pray

Dear God, it makes me feel

....

when I am chosen to do

....

1 Samuel 16; 2 Samuel 5:1–5

What are people like?

Daddy had taken the twins to see his uncle. Lucy and Liam were very quiet. On the way home Daddy said, "Why didn't you speak to Uncle Henry or thank him when he gave you those presents? That was very rude."

"But he walks funny," said Liam.

"And he talks funny," said Lucy.

"That's because he's not very well. He's got a disease, which means he can't talk or walk like we can," explained Daddy.

"God says, **'People judge others by what they look like, but I judge people by what is in their hearts.'** Uncle Henry is very kind and thoughtful. He knew just what you would both like. Wasn't he clever to get you a dumper truck, Liam? And to remember you like dressing up, Lucy. You can be a real princess with your new tiara."

Pray

Thank you for kind people, God. Sometimes I see people who look different, help me to be kind to them.

1 Samuel 16; 2 Samuel 5:1–5

At Reese's house

The twins were at Reese's house. Reese's Auntie Marlene cooked them some special food.

"Yum," said Reese. "Jerk Chicken, my favourite."

"Ugh," said Lucy. "It hurts my mouth!"

Auntie Marlene smiled, "Sorry, Lucy. I forgot to say it's spicy. We like spicy food in Jamaica where my family comes from."

Have you tried food from another country? Did you like it?

Daniel had been taken to a far-off country to serve in the king's palace. "Teach Daniel to speak our language," said the king. "Give him the same food as me." Daniel knew God wouldn't want him to eat that sort of food. God made the man in charge friendly to Daniel. The man let Daniel eat different food for a while. He soon saw that Daniel's food made him healthier than everyone else.

Pray

Talk about the food that people eat in different parts of the world. Some people don't have enough to eat. Ask God to give them food.

The king's dream

Liam ran into Mummy's room. "I had a bad dream!" he
sobbed.

Have you ever had a bad dream?

One night, King Nebuchadnezzar had a dream.

"Tell me what my dream was and what it meant," he said
to his wise men.

"But that's impossible!" they answered.

"Then you will all die!" the king said
angrily.

Daniel bowed before the king, "Give me
time, I will explain your dream."

Daniel went home and asked his friends
to pray. While Daniel was asleep, God
explained the dream to him.

Daniel went straight to the king.

"Your majesty, the cleverest person in
the world couldn't do what you have
asked. Only God who rules from heaven can explain
mysteries."

The king was amazed when Daniel explained the dream.

Pray

Dear God, thank you for helping Daniel.
When I go to bed please give me good
dreams too.

Daniel hears God

Lucy and Liam are looking for special clothes in the dressing-up box so they can be Daniel and the king.

"I'll be the king," says Lucy, finding a crown and a shiny green dress.

"These are clothes for a wise man," says Liam, pulling out silky Chinese pyjamas.

Daniel told King Nebuchadnezzar everything that God had said to him in the dream.

"Your Majesty, the great God has told you what is going to happen in the future."

The king was amazed. He said, "Now I know that your God is greater than all other gods and kings, because he gave you the power to explain this mystery."

The king was so pleased that he gave Daniel lots of gifts and put him in charge of all the other wise men.

Pray

Dear God, you knew all about the king's dream. You know what will happen tomorrow.

I'm glad you know everything.

The right answer?
Talking with young children

Have you ever noticed how often we ask questions when we talk to children?
• Have you got any brothers or sisters?
• What are you doing?
It's very easy to slip into 'management' mode and spend our time telling children what to do, how to do it and then asking questions to see whether it's been done. How much of what we say is 'managing' the children and how much is conversational? Maybe we need to change our questions to include those that put us alongside our children:
• Would you like to see what I've put out for you to play with?
• What kind of food do you like best?
Listen carefully to a TV chat-show and see how the interviewer draws out the guests by using 'open' questions. Try it with a child. 'Do you like playgroup?' closes down conversation, because the answer can only be yes or no. 'What happens at playgroup?' allows for several possible replies and the child can give a more informative answer. It's risky because we may not get the answer we want or expect. But learning is more than being given 'right answers'. It's about beginning to think for oneself. This opens up the ability to 'wonder' about things as we grow up: who God is; who we are; about suffering.

All great Christian thinkers have looked beyond the 'obvious' and what is thought to be 'correct', to trust in their own ability to have deep insights into the Christian faith. We have the opportunity to encourage young children to begin to think for themselves. It's one small way in which we can help them grow in faith, opening their minds to the riches that God wants them to discover and enjoy.